Broken and Blessed

How God Used One Imperfect Family to Change the World

Jessica LaGrone

A Bible Study on Genesis

Leader Guide
Jenny Youngman, Contributor

ABINGDON PRESS

Nashville

BROKEN AND BLESSED:
HOW GOD USED ONE IMPERFECT FAMILY
TO CHANGE THE WORLD

LEADER GUIDE

Copyright © 2014 Abingdon Press

This book is printed on acid-free paper.

ISBN 978-1-4267-7838-4

14 15 16 17 18 19 20 21 22 23—10 9 8 7 6 5 4 3 2 1
MANUFACTURED IN THE UNITED STATES OF AMERICA

Contents

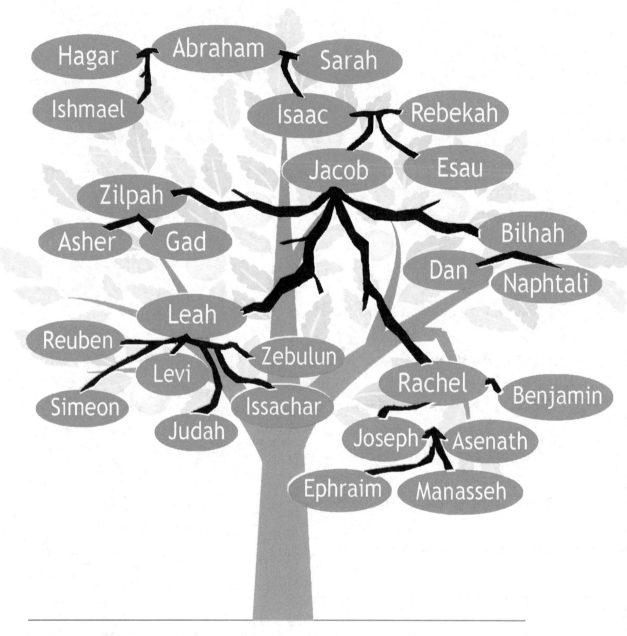

Abraham's Family Tree

Introduction

The book of Genesis traces the branches of a single, perfectly imperfect family and God's constant and unfailing love for them. It serves as a kind of scrapbook for this family, recording both the good and bad pictures of their experiences. Part of the beauty of this family's story is that, while they are not perfect, they were chosen by God for a specific purpose. They are both broken and blessed.

As I began to read the Genesis narrative as a family story, it helped me to understand that God doesn't wait for us to be perfect before loving us. I decided that if God chose to use this unusual family for His purposes, then maybe He wants to use me and my family to change the world, too.

When we flip forward in the Bible's family scrapbook to the New Testament, we find our own pictures there. Galatians promises us that because we belong to Christ, we are now part of the Genesis family, heirs to all the promises of blessing God made to Abraham and Sarah and their family long ago (Galatians 3:29). Now when we read Genesis, we can do so with the realization that this is our story, our family, and the origin of our own brokenness and blessing.

This study invites you to discover the roots of our biblical family tree. It leads us to ask the question, "Could God use my family to change the world?" As we study together, we'll learn that because the title "Child of God" belongs to us, this Genesis family is our family. And because of that, we are infinitely more blessed than broken.

About the Participant Book

Before the first session, you will want to distribute copies of the participant book to the members of your group. Be sure to communicate that they are to complete the first week of readings *before* your first group session. Or you may choose to have an introductory session and hand out books at that time. For each week there are five readings that feature the following components:

Read God's Word	A portion of the Bible story for the week, occasionally with other Scripture readings.
Reflect and Respond	A guided reflection and study of the Scripture with space for recording your responses.

Pray About It	A sample prayer to guide you into a personal time of prayer.
Act On It	Ideas to help you act on what you have read.

Completing these readings each week will prepare the women for the discussion and activities of the group session.

About This Leader Guide

As you gather each week with your group, you will have the opportunity to watch a video, discuss and respond to what you're learning, and pray together. You will need access to a television and DVD player with working remotes.

Creating an inviting atmosphere will help to make the women feel welcome. Although optional, you might consider providing snacks for your first meeting and inviting group members to rotate in bringing refreshments each week.

This leader guide and the DVD will be your primary tools for leading each session. In this book you will find outlines for six group sessions, plus an optional introductory session. The introductory session is 60 minutes; all other sessions have two format options:

60-Minute Format

Preparing Your Hearts and Minds	2 minutes
Getting to Know Each Other	3-5 minutes
Video	25-30 minutes
Group Discussion	20 minutes
Closing Prayer	3 minutes

90-Minute Format

Preparing Your Hearts and Minds	2 minutes
Getting to Know Each Other	3-5 minutes
Video	25-30 minutes
Group Discussion	25 minutes
*Act On It	10 minutes
*Group Activity	15 minutes
Closing Prayer	3 minutes

As you can see, the 90-minute format is identical to the 60-minute format but has a slightly longer discussion time plus two additional segments, which are marked above with an asterisk. Feel free to adapt or modify either of these formats, as well as the individual segments and activities, in any way to meet the specific needs and preferences of your group.

Here is a brief overview of the elements included in both formats:

Leader Prep (Before the Session)

For your preparation prior to the group session, this section provides an overview of the week's Bible story, a recap of the weekly readings, a list of materials and equipment needed, and a teaching objective. Be sure to read this section, as well as the session outline, before the group session. If you choose, you also may find it helpful to review the DVD segment in advance.

Preparing Your Hearts and Minds (2 minutes)

You may find that participants are rushed and distracted as they arrive at Bible study (yourself included). You've had to pull away from your busy lives, schedules, and families to get there. Playing a quiet, meaningful song as everyone gathers will allow you to disconnect from the outside world and center your hearts on God. (One recommendation is to play a portion of the song "Blessings" by Laura Story. The full song is over four minutes.) Bring an iPod with speakers or a CD player and CD. After the song has ended, pray the opening prayer that is provided or one of your own.

Getting to Know Each Other (3-5 minutes)

Use the get-to-know-you activity to engage the women in the topic while helping them to feel comfortable with one another.

Video (25-30 minutes)

Next, watch the week's video segment together. Be sure to direct participants to the Video Viewer Guide in the participant book, which they may complete as they watch the video.

Group Discussion (20-25 minutes depending on session length)

After watching the video, use the discussion points and questions provided to facilitate group discussion. You may choose to read aloud the discussion points or express them in your own words; then use one or more of the questions that follow to guide your conversation.

Note that more discussion points and questions have been provided than you will have time to include. Before the session, select those you want to cover, and put a check mark beside them. Reflect on each question and make some notes in the margins to share during your discussion time. Questions highlighted in bold may be found in the participant book. (Brackets indicate changes so questions will make sense when read aloud to the group.) For these questions, you may want to invite participants to share the answers they wrote in their own books.

Depending on the number of women in your group and the level of their participation, you may not have time to cover everything you have selected, and that is OK. Rather than attempting to bulldoze through, follow the Spirit's lead and be open to where He takes the conversation. Remember that your role is not to have all of the answers but to encourage discussion and sharing.

*Act On It (10 minutes)

If your group is meeting for 90 minutes, invite each woman to turn to a neighbor and discuss one or more challenges from the Act On It section of the weekly readings. This will encourage the women to apply what they are learning as well as provide some accountability. If possible, try to come back together as a full group for the last few minutes of this segment to share some responses.

*Group Activity (15 minutes)

If you are meeting for 90 minutes, move to the group activity, which involves participants in active learning. (Be sure to collect any necessary items in advance.)

Closing Prayer (3 minutes)

Close by leading the group in prayer. Invite the women to briefly name prayer requests. To get things started, you might share a personal request of your own. As women share, model for the group by writing each request in your participant book, indicating that you will remember to pray for them during the week.

As the study progresses, encourage members to participate in the closing prayer by praying out loud for each other and the requests given. Ask the women to volunteer to pray for specific requests, or have each woman pray for the woman on her right or left. Make sure nametags are visible so that group members do not feel awkward if they do not remember someone's name. After the prayer, remind the women to pray for one another throughout the week.

Group Mission Project

As part of this study, you are encouraged to involve your group in a mission project focused on blessing children, women, and/or families who need to know that they belong to God's family. Prior to your first session, do some research on local children's homes, women's shelters, or family outreach programs. Suggest several possibilities for the group to choose from.

After choosing a group or organization, discuss and plan what you can do to serve them. Again, it is helpful to provide a few choices; or you might want to invite a few volunteers to meet outside of group time to make plans. If you choose a local children's home, you might work with the home to plan a collection drive for new clothes, toys, and books; throw a birthday party for the children (or plan monthly birthday parties); provide tutoring; or meet other needs. If you choose a women's shelter, family outreach program, or other organization, contact them to assess their needs and plan a collection drive, service day, or specific projects such as providing a training session on job search tips and techniques, computer skills, financial planning and budgeting, or some other topic. If collecting items, gather them over the course of your study and then, at the end of the study, pray a blessing over them and send them off. If planning a service day or other project, put it on the calendar at the beginning of the study and remind the group through verbal announcements and e-mail as the date approaches. A group mission project is a great way to provide an opportunity for women to respond to the study's message that we have been blessed to be a blessing.

You also are encouraged to share your group mission project with other women's groups by sending a description of the project along with photos to news@abingdonwomen.com. We will share these on AbingdonWomen.com as well as through social media.

Before You Begin

It has been said that there are three keys to a successful study: (1) prayer, (2) preparation, and (3) personalization. Pray for each and every member of your group by name, pray for each session, and pray for God to use you as His instrument. Do your homework by completing the readings and preparing for each session well in advance of your meeting time. And as I've already mentioned, be sure to personalize the study to match your teaching style and/or to meet the needs and interests of your group. Some groups are more discussion oriented and may want to increase discussion time and omit the Group Activity. Others may choose to abbreviate Group Discussion to allow more time for the hands-on activity or closing prayer time. Feel free to make it your own.

May God richly bless your time together as you study His Word and discover how you have been blessed to be a blessing!

Leader Helps

- Communicate dates and times to participants in advance.
- Distribute books at least one week before your first session or during an introductory session. Instruct the women to complete the first week's readings prior to Week 1's session. If you have contact information, send out a reminder and a welcome.
- Be sure the meeting space is ready before each group session. (See the list of materials needed in each session outline.)
- Pray for your group and each group member by name.
- Read and complete the week's readings in the participant book and review the session outline in this leader guide. Select the discussion points and questions you want to cover and make some notes in the margins.
- Welcome and greet each woman as she arrives.
- Ask the women to turn off or silence their cell phones.
- Encourage participation, but don't put anyone on the spot. Offer a personal example or answer if no one else responds at first.
- Communicate the importance of completing the weekly readings and participating in Group Discussion.
- Facilitate but don't dominate. If someone else monopolizes the conversation, kindly thank her for sharing and ask if anyone else has any insights.
- Try not to interrupt, judge, or minimize anyone's comments or input.
- Acknowledge that you're on this journey together, with the Holy Spirit as your leader. If issues or questions arise that you don't feel equipped to handle or answer, talk with your pastor or a church staff member.
- Don't rush to fill the silence. If no one speaks right away, it's okay to wait for someone to answer. After a moment, ask, "Would anyone be willing to share?" If no one responds, try asking the question again a different way—or offer a brief response and ask if anyone has anything to add.
- Encourage discussion, but don't hesitate to call time on a question and move ahead to stay on track. If you spend extra time on a given question or activity, consider skipping or spending less time on another question.
- End on time. Thank the women for coming and let them know you're looking forward to seeing them next time.
- Be prepared for some women to hang out and talk at the end. If you need everyone to leave by a certain time, communicate this at the beginning of the group session.

Introductory Session

Leader Prep

Note: The regular session outline has been modified for this optional introductory session and is 60 minutes long.

What You Will Need

- iPod or MP3 player with speakers or CD player and CD (see Preparing Your Hearts and Minds)
- *Broken and Blessed* DVD and DVD player
- Stick-on nametags and markers
- Group mission project information (create a handout or provide brochures from various organizations)

Session Objective

Today you will introduce your group to God's plan for the Genesis family.

Session Outline

Preparing Your Hearts and Minds (2 minutes)

To help the women disconnect from the outside world and center their hearts on God, play a quiet, meaningful song as they are gathering. After the song has ended, pray the opening prayer below or a prayer of your own.

> *Loving God,*
> *Thank You for this opportunity to study Your Word. As we learn about the Genesis family, may we also discover how You can bring blessing from brokenness in our own lives. In Jesus' name we pray. Amen.*

Getting to Know Each Other (3-5 minutes)

Hand out participant books as well as nametags and markers, and ask participants to write their names and wear the nametags for the session. Then ask each woman to find a partner and briefly share why she chose this study and what she hopes to gain from it. After a couple of minutes, come back together and invite a few volunteers to share with the full group.

Video (about 15 minutes)

Play the Introductory Session video segment on the DVD. Invite participants to complete the Video Viewer Guide for the Introductory Session in the participant book as they watch.

Group Discussion (20 minutes)

Note that more discussion points and questions have been provided than you will have time to include. Before the session, select those you want to cover, and put a check mark beside them.

1. Family is about having people who will always love you enough to give you another chance. Families are what God invented to show us how He feels about us. We only understand God's love because someone with skin on loved us first.
   - How have you experienced family as a group of people who love you enough to give you another chance?
   - Who has demonstrated the love of God in your life?

2. When God wants to change the world, He starts with a family. God pours blessings into our lives so that they may overflow and heal the rest of the world. We are blessed to be a blessing.
   - What does it mean to say that the family is a powerful "secret weapon"?
   - What is God's purpose for the family?
   - In what ways have you and your family been blessed to be a blessing?

3. There is no such thing as the perfect family. When God wants to change a family, He starts with one person.
   - Have you ever felt that your family is "less than" because you have issues? Why is it important to acknowledge that all of our families are broken? What are some appropriate ways we can do this in the church?
   - Has there ever been someone in your family who made a decision to change, affecting generations to come?

4. Family is not some place we come to at the end of the day after our work is done. Family is our most important work.
   • In what ways does it encourage or challenge you to know that the family is your most important work?

5. God sent His Son to be born into Abraham and Sarah's family—into a generation no more perfect than any other—and Jesus opened up this family to anyone who believes in Him. He invites us into this family, now called the church. It's the job of the church family to tell and show others how much they are loved so that they can understand the unseen love of God.
   • What did God do to make it possible for us to become part of His family?
   • In what ways is your church the arms and feet of Jesus?
   • What is your important part to play in God's family, and how can you fulfill it?

Group Activity (15 minutes)

Explain to the group that as you gather to study Genesis and discover what it means to be a member of God's family, you will be working together on a mission project to bless children, women, and/or families who need to know they, too, belong to God's family. Provide information and materials (such as brochures or a handout) about several organizations, programs, or houses/centers and the various needs that you might address together. If you choose a local children's home, you might work with the home to plan a collection drive for new clothes, toys, and books and throw a birthday party for the children. If you choose a women's shelter, family outreach program, or other organization, you might consider a collection drive or service day. Discuss the options and decide together what you would like to do or, if you prefer, invite a few volunteers to meet outside of group time to make plans. If you choose to collect items, have participants bring them each week throughout the study and then, at your last session, pray a blessing over them and send them off. If you choose to have a service event or activity, set a date and remind the group, through verbal announcements and e-mail, as the date approaches.

Closing Prayer (3 minutes)

In preparation for next week, invite participants to bring a family album or scrapbook with them—of either their family of origin, their current family, or their family of choice (close friends who are like family). Close the session by leading the group in prayer. Let participants know that as you continue meeting together, you will invite them to share prayer requests and encourage them to participate by praying out loud for each other and the requests named.

Week 1
Adam and Eve

Leader Prep

Bible Story Overview

This week we begin at the beginning. It's the beginning of time, space, order, hierarchy, beings, and blessing. When God created the world, He had a big idea. He would separate sky and land. He would paint the sky blue and texturize the land and sea with varying hues and landscapes. He would make marvelous creatures—too many to number. And then, His great big idea: human beings—not just independent human beings, but a family.

The family, Adam and Eve, began their life together in harmony with each other and with God. This season in time was perfection. But then it wasn't. A serpent appeared in their perfect home and tempted Eve through deception, and she listened. She and Adam sinned, and as sin entered the world, everything changed. Suddenly there was brokenness in their relationship with the environment, their relationship with each other, and their relationship with God. But God, who is always good and always ready to offer grace and second chances, had a plan to turn their brokenness into blessing.

Weekly Readings Recap

Review the key themes of the week:

Day 1: From the beginning we see that God and darkness are at odds with each other. God will not let darkness rule the earth. Where there is darkness in our lives, in our families, and in our world, God is there, ready to act and bring light and love in places of trouble and despair.

Day 2: The first chapter of Genesis is dedicated to God building a home—our world. This home was prepared for us with purpose and care by a Bridegroom who longed to live in it side by side with the bride He was creating for Himself.

Day 3: We are made in God's image. We are made with a connection to our home (environment) and to our Creator. We are made for each other.

Day 4: God's response to sin is grace. When we make wrong choices and sin, God loves us just the same.

Day 5: Sin resulted in consequences that brought brokenness to human beings' relationship with God, their environment, and each other. Yet God never gives up on His children. God's grace always spreads further than the reach of any sin. We are never outside the reach of God's love.

What You Will Need

- iPod or MP3 player with speakers or CD player and CD (see Preparing Your Hearts and Minds)
- *Broken and Blessed* DVD and DVD player
- Stick-on nametags and markers
- Group mission project information (for groups that did not have an Introductory Session; create a handout—recommended for a 60-minute session—or provide brochures from various organizations)

Session Objective

Today you will help the women in your group to realize that they belong to God's family and, despite their brokenness, are covered by His grace.

Session Outline

Preparing Your Hearts and Minds (2 minutes)

To help the women disconnect from the outside world and center their hearts on God, play a quiet, meaningful song as they are gathering. After the song has ended, pray the opening prayer below or a prayer of your own.

> *Creator God,*
> *What a privilege to be in Your family! We are blessed beyond understanding that You are mindful of us, that You created us, that You love*

us, that You forgive us, that You bless us in so many ways. Come meet with us now and write Your word on our hearts. In Jesus' name we pray. Amen.

Getting to Know Each Other (3-5 minutes)

Hand out nametags and markers and ask participants to write their names and wear the nametags for the session. Then ask each woman to find a partner. Tell them that they are going to share with their partners a one-minute version of their family background or history. Explain that you'll announce when one minute is up, and then it will be the other partner's turn. Some ladies will want to talk more than time will allow, and some will be stumped about what to say. The point is for them to share only the major highlights. (For example, I might share that my parents divorced when I was one year old, and then both remarried and redivorced by the time I was in middle school. My mom did a great job of raising me in a single-parent home, and the church provided a wonderful extended family for me. Now I'm married and have two small children.)

After a couple of minutes, come back together as a full group and have each woman quickly introduce her partner to the group telling the partner's name and some highlight from her family history.

Video (25-30 minutes)

Play the Week 1 video segment on the DVD. Invite participants to complete the Video Viewer Guide for Week 1 in the participant book as they watch.

Group Discussion (20-25 minutes)

Note that more discussion points and questions have been provided than you will have time to include. Before the session, select those you want to cover, and put a check mark beside them. Questions highlighted in bold are from the participant book. (In some instances, changes have been made, indicated with brackets, so that the questions make sense when read aloud to the group.) For these questions, you may want to invite participants to share the answers they wrote in their books.

1. **Review and summarize the story of Tara. (Day 1)**
   - Why do you think we have such an innate desire to know where we come from?
   - If we went back on our family trees as far as we could go, all the way back to the beginning, what would we find?

2. From the beginning we see that God and darkness are at odds with each other. God will not let darkness rule the earth. Where there is darkness in our lives, in our families, and in our world, we can be assured that God is speaking there, working to bring light in places of trouble and despair. (Day 1 and Video)
   - Have someone read aloud Genesis 1:3 and 1 John 1:5. Based on these verses, what is God's job description?
   - How does God invite us to join in this job description, and what role does the family play?

3. In the best of circumstances, families are the instruments through which God forms, fills, and lights our existence. In the worst circumstances, we find in them chaos, emptiness, and darkness. If we are honest, all of our families are the framework by which we live out the worst and best moments in our lives. There is nothing closer, nothing more personal, nothing that pushes our emotional buttons more—for good and bad—than our families. (Day 1)
   - **How has your family formed you?**
   - **What did your family fill you with or instill in you?**
   - **Has there been a time when family (blood-related or chosen) has been a light in the dark world for you?**

4. Days 1-3 of the Creation story show God preparing an environment, a home; days 4-6 describe its inhabitants, the creatures who will live there. (Day 2)
   - What does this insight tell you about the nature of God?
   - What are some examples in your own life of creating a welcoming space first and then filling the space with guests?

5. God separates the last day from the previous six. He makes it different by not working. He creates it by not creating. The text tells us that He makes the seventh day "holy." (Day 2)
   - Have someone read Genesis 2:2-3. Why do you think God marks a day by not creating?
   - **What is this a day for?**
   - **Describe how you can honor the Sabbath that God created on the seventh day.**
   - **What does it feel like when you spend time at rest with God?**

6. We are God's masterpiece. If God has picture frames hanging around heaven, they are filled with the human family. And every one of us is made to look like Him. (Day 3)

- Have some volunteers read Psalm 116:5, Philippians 2:6-7, Colossians 3:13, and 1 John 4:8. What do these passages tell us about our resemblance to God?
- **As image-bearers of our Creator, what are the attributes of God that we can display?**

7. Humans aren't just the inhabitants, filling the environment of earth. We're also an environment created for the One Holy Inhabitant to occupy, filling us with His image, His breath. (Day 3)
   - **What does 1 Corinthians 6:19-20 tell us about ourselves?**
   - What does it mean to be a temple for the Lord?
   - **What does it suggest should be our response?**

8. Review the definition of *ezer*. We are made for each other. Humans are created to help other humans, to be *ezers* to them. (Day 3)
   - How is God our *ezer*?
   - How are we to be *ezers* to each other?
   - **What instructions do we find in Philippians 2:3-4?**

9. Review the introduction of the serpent to the garden and Eve's and Adam's actions afterward. Sin often proceeds from deception, from believing untruths about God or ourselves. (Day 4)
   - How did sin proceed from deception for Eve?
   - When has sin proceeded from deception in your life?

10. After the act of sin and the shame that followed, Adam and Eve stand before God, vulnerable, exposed, naked, and ashamed. Will He be wrathful? Angry? Cold? Rejecting? (Day 4 and Video)
    - **How would you describe God's response to their sin?**
    - What is God's response to our sin?
    - How is God like a parent calling out for a lost child? What does this tell us about God?
    - **What truth about God reassures you when you've messed up?**

11. When the woman tasted the forbidden fruit and offered it to her husband, who did the same, it didn't take long for those relationships to sting with the consequences of their actions. (Day 5 and Video)
    - **Review Genesis 3:14-19 and describe the consequences for each [of the following: serpent, woman, man].**

12. There has been debate through the years about whether the original consequences found in Genesis 2 are gender specific or not. Certainly both

parents experience pain related to their children. Both men and women inherit the consequences of unequal relationships and power struggles. Both sexes can suffer the consequences of having to toil for their livelihood. Yet a casual survey of friends often suggests that women tend to wrestle more with the pangs of relationship issues and men tend to grapple more with how their identity and their work are bound together. (Day 5)

- What about you? Do you feel the consequences given in Genesis 3 are gender specific, or do you think the entire list affects the whole of the human race?

13. Wrap up Group Discussion with these questions:
    - What surprised you as you studied the Creation story? What did you learn?
    - What did you learn this week about God? About yourself?
    - How does it impact your life to realize that you belong to God's family and are covered by His grace?

*Act On It (10 minutes)

If you are meeting for 90 minutes, ask everyone to turn to a neighbor and talk about one or more of the following challenges from the Act On It section of the weekly readings:

Day 1: Tell of your experience of calling or writing an older relative and asking him or her to tell you a story about the family—or your experience of looking through some old pictures or letters and taking a moment to remember those stories yourself. Where do you see God at work in your family's past?

Day 2: Talk about the time you spent in God's creation. Where did you see the grandness of God? Where did you see His care for the smallest specifics of creation?

Day 5: Discuss what happened when you asked others to tell you about their families.

If possible, try to come back together for the last few minutes of this segment and invite a few volunteers to share their responses to one of the questions.

*Group Activity (15 minutes)

If you are meeting for 90 minutes and did not hold an Introductory Session, explain to the group that as you gather to study Genesis and discover what it means to be a member of God's family, you will be working together on a mission project to bless children, women, and/or families who need to know they, too, belong to God's family. Provide information and materials (such as brochures or a handouts) about several organizations, programs, or houses/centers and the various needs that you might address together. If you choose a local children's home, you might work with the home to plan a collection drive for new clothes, toys, and books and throw a birthday party for the children. If you choose a women's shelter, family outreach program, or other organization, you might consider a collection drive or service day. Discuss the options and decide together what you would like to do, or you might prefer to invite a few volunteers to meet outside of group time to make plans. If you choose to collect items, have participants bring them each week throughout the study and then, at your last session, pray a blessing over them and send them off. If you choose to have a service event or activity, set a date and remind the group, through verbal announcements and e-mail, as the date approaches.

If you are meeting for 90 minutes and did hold an Introductory Session, invite the women to get out the family albums or scrapbooks that they brought with them and spend time mingling, browsing, and talking together further about their family backgrounds and experiences.

Closing Prayer (3 minutes)

If you are meeting for 60 minutes and did not hold an Introductory Session, take just a moment before prayer to explain the group mission project and present possibilities. Prepare a handout in advance outlining several options for the women to take home and consider; then you can decide together next week what you will do. Or you might decide to have a few volunteers plan outside the group session on behalf of the entire group.

If you are meeting for 60 minutes and did hold an introductory session, have the women vote for a project by a show of hands. Select a few volunteers to begin making specific plans outside of class on behalf of the group.

Close the session by taking personal prayer requests from group members and leading the group in prayer. As you progress to later weeks in the study, encourage members to participate in the closing prayer by praying out loud for each other and the requests given. Remind group members to pray for one another throughout the week.

Week 2
Abraham and Sarah

Leader Prep

Bible Story Overview

Isn't it oddly wonderful to find out that someone you revere or put on a pedestal is actually a normal person like yourself? This week we found out that some of our Bible heroes, the ones we learned in our children's Bibles were pillars of our faith, were actually real, failure-prone human beings who needed God's grace and mercy just as much as we do.

When sin entered the world, the perfect relationship with God and with one another was no longer part of the story. But God used imperfect families all along the way to bring about His will. In fact, God blessed one family in particular, Abraham's family, so that they would be a blessing to many. Despite poor choices and challenges on the journey, they were blessed to be a blessing, and so are we.

Weekly Readings Recap

Review the key themes of the week:

Day 1: The pattern that Genesis reveals is that where sin is concerned, what starts small spreads out and takes over. From Genesis 3 to 11, humanity brushes off God's guidance and walks its own path. The first part of the Bible establishes the great problem of humanity before it answers with God's solution. We must understand how truly broken we are before we can understand just how remarkable God's response of blessing is.

Day 2: When God wants to change the world, He starts with a family. God re-forms our families so that we can be conduits of His blessings.

Day 3: Easy circumstances are no proof of God's blessing. Difficult ones are no indication of His absence. As you travel in and out of the desert seasons of your life, remember that God travels with you. You are never alone.

Day 4: Abraham's gift is not that he has a perfect faith but that he has a perfect God. Like Abraham, our transgressions are great, our sins deserve punishment, and we break our end of the covenant; but God is still holding up His end. In fact, God is keeping both His and our end of the covenant.

Day 5: You and I have been given precious gifts in our families and in our lives. The story of Isaac's near sacrifice reminds us that when we are tempted to worry about our loved ones, to hold them too tightly, to try to play god in their lives, we need to remember that the Giver of all good and perfect gifts loves them far more than we can imagine.

What You Will Need

- iPod or MP3 player with speakers or CD player and CD (see Preparing Your Hearts and Minds)
- *Broken and Blessed* DVD and DVD player
- Stick-on nametags and markers
- Brown, dark green, and light green construction paper
- Scissors, glue, pencils, and pens
- A copy of the family tree patterns for each participant (see pages 62 and 63)

Session Objective

Today you will help the women in your group embrace God's mercy and grace as they grow in their trust and obedience to God.

Session Outline

Preparing Your Hearts and Minds (2 minutes)

To help the women disconnect from the outside world and center their hearts on God, play a quiet, meaningful song as they are gathering. After the song has ended, pray the following opening prayer or a prayer of your own.

Father God,

Once again we remember that You have called us by name, that we belong to You. As we gather to study Your Word and discover our place in the story You've been writing through all of history, open our hearts and minds to what You would teach us. Reveal new insights to us about who You are and who we are in You. In Jesus' name we pray. Amen.

Getting to Know Each Other (3-5 minutes)

Hand out nametags and markers and ask participants to write their names and wear the nametags for the session. Then have the women form small groups of three to four. Ask them how young they were when they were first exposed to the Bible and what they remember learning about various Bible stories—perhaps from a children's Bible. You might need to help them start with some questions like these:

- How early do you remember hearing a Bible story?
- How old were you when you first owned a Bible? Did you ever have a children's Bible?
- What do you remember about the Bible stories you heard or read?
- Who was your favorite Bible character as a child? Why?
- What are some details you discovered about Noah and Abraham this week that a children's Bible might leave out?

After a couple of minutes, come back together as a full group and have the women share the highlights from their conversations.

Video (25-30 minutes)

Play the Week 2 video segment on the DVD. Invite participants to complete the Video Viewer Guide for Week 2 in the participant book as they watch.

Group Discussion (20-25 minutes)

Note that more discussion points and questions have been provided than you will have time to include. Before the session, select those you want to cover, and put a check mark beside them. Questions highlighted in bold are from the participant book. (In some instances, changes have been made, indicated with brackets, so that the questions make sense when read aloud to the group.) For these questions, you may want to invite participants to share the answers they wrote in their books.

1. The world's introduction to sin was represented by something so small, so seemingly insignificant. It was just one tiny piece of fruit. But here, at the beginning of human history, is what the Bible teaches about sin: a little bit can go a long way. (Day 1)
   • Sin began with a piece of fruit; only one generation later it became murder and then, in time, a completely corrupt humanity. **What does Genesis 6:5-6 tell us?**
   • Who was the only bright spot in the human family picture?

2. When we try to rule the world on our own, chaos breaks out again. Emptiness reigns. Darkness falls. The good news is that while we live in a volatile and erratic world, God is predictable. Wherever there is chaos, we can always expect to find God at work creating order, stability, and wholeness. (Day 1)
   • Where have you seen God at work bringing order, stability, and wholeness?
   • Noah is introduced in the story as the only righteous man among all of humanity. What had happened to his family by the end of his biblical episode?
   • From fruit to ark, from Noah's binge to Babel, Genesis is up front with us, providing a clear picture of what happens to humanity when we are left to our own devices. What is the humorous name given for Genesis Chapter 11? Why is this name appropriate?

3. Genesis 12 takes a turn away from the corruption and sin of Chapter 11 and brings us into new territory with Abram and Sarai. These two who are called to journey to a new home will become the fami ly through whom God intends to bless His people. (Day 2 and Video)
   • Have someone read Genesis 12:1-3. **What are God's instructions and promises to Abram?**
   • What is significant about God's promise to make Abram a "blessing" to others?
   • What is the cost of Abram and Sarai's calling? What did they have to leave behind?
   • **How would you describe the unwritten script handed down by your family? What parts of this script do you want to continue living out? What parts might God be calling you to leave behind or rewrite?**

4. There's something you notice right away about this family God is calling to change the world: They're not perfect. (Day 3)
   • Why do you think God uses imperfect people to accomplish His work in the world?

- Who are some imperfect people who have done significant good in the world?
- How has God used your imperfections to work in you and others?

5. Abraham and Sarah are a great reminder for us of these truths: Easy circumstances are no proof of God's blessing. Difficult circumstances are no indication of His absence. (Day 3)
   - How has this been true in your own life?
   - How was this true for Abraham and Sarah?

6. When Sarah lacks trust in God's faithfulness, she takes matters into her own hands. (Day 3 and Video)
   - What is Eve's legacy that Sarah—and every woman since—has inherited?
   - Review the details of Sarah and Hagar's story (Genesis Chapters 16 and 21). **What is Sarah's [first] plan?**
   - What are the results of her great idea, and is she happy with the results?
   - **What is Sarah's [second] plan?**
   - In the video we heard this statement: If our pain isn't transformed, it will end up being transferred. How was this true in Sarah's story? How has it been true in your own life?

7. Despite Sarah's scheming, God remains in control of the situation and redeems it. (Day 3 and Video)
   - How does God redeem the situation?
   - What does this teach us about God? How can this encourage us when we find ourselves in the desert?
   - Read aloud Psalm 46:10. What instruction does this verse give us for those times when we are worried or struggling to manipulate and control circumstances or people?

8. For all of his faith and trust in God, Abraham had brief episodes of unbelief. (Day 4)
   - Review Genesis 12 and 20. What lie does Abraham tell—repeatedly?
   - Why does he put on this charade?

9. Abraham doesn't have it all right, but he gets at least one thing right. He has faith in the right God. Your faith may seem pretty imperfect on some days. You may fail to do the things you know you should. You may do the things you know you shouldn't. If that's the case, welcome to the family—a family full of perfectly loved children. Because of Father Abraham, you can know that your imperfect faith is enough because it is based in our perfect, covenant God. (Day 4)

- How has your faith been imperfect at times?
- How can we achieve the kind of faith in God that Abraham had?

10. If calling Sarah his sister displayed a little lack of trust, Abraham would later outdo himself in a display of faith that many of us cannot imagine. With Isaac, their heart's desire, in their arms, Abraham and Sarah would be tested to see who would hold center stage in their lives and decision making. (Day 5)
   - Have some volunteers read Genesis 22:1-19. **What does God ask Abraham to do?**
   - What do you think went through Abraham's mind on the way to the mountain?
   - Why do you think God tested Abraham in this way?
   - What does this story teach us about God?
   - Do you completely trust God with your most precious gifts? Why or why not?

11. Wrap up Group Discussion with these questions:
   - What did you discover about brokenness and blessing this week?
   - What did you learn this week about God? About yourself?
   - How does it affect your life to discover that you are blessed to be a blessing?

*Act On It (10 minutes)

If you are meeting for 90 minutes, ask everyone to turn to a neighbor and talk about one or more of the following challenges from the Act On It section of the weekly readings:

Day 2: Tell about your experience of taking a blessings inventory. Name some of your most treasured blessings. What surprised you about God's blessings in your life? How is God using your blessings to bless others?

Day 4: Explain how it has affected you to realize that your gift is not a perfect faith but a perfect God.

Day 5: Talk about your experience of praying to let go of control over someone you tend to hold too tightly. Were you able to surrender control to our perfect God?

If possible, try to come back together for the last few minutes of this segment and invite a few volunteers to share their responses to one of the questions.

*Group Activity (15 minutes)

If you are meeting for 90 minutes, provide sheets of dark green, light green, brown, and white construction paper, as well as pencils and pens, scissors, and glue. Also provide copies of the family tree patterns (see pages 62-63). Explain that each person is to create her own family tree by tracing, cutting out, and assembling the pattern pieces on a sheet of white construction paper. Instruct them to include as many family members or generations as they can from memory (without doing any research), writing one name on each leaf. After gluing the leaves on the tree in the appropriate order (traditionally maternal relatives are on the ride side and paternal on the left, with husbands and wives side by side and children below), have them draw connecting lines. As they work, ask the following questions:

- What are some family traits and characteristics that have been passed down through every generation?
- Is there a physical trait that is common among your family members?
- What are you most thankful for about your family heritage?

When they are finished, encourage them to take home their family trees, frame them, and set them on a dresser or bookshelf as a reminder to give thanks each day that their family tree extends all the way back to our Creator.

Closing Prayer (3 minutes)

If you are meeting for 60 minutes and did not hold an Introductory Session, briefly recap the options for the group mission project. Have the women vote for a project by a show of hands. Select a few volunteers to begin making specific plans outside of class on behalf of the group.

In preparation for next week, instruct each group member to bring an item that she inherited from a previous generation in the family. If the item is too large or fragile, she may bring a picture of the item.

Close the session by taking personal prayer requests from group members and leading the group in prayer. As you progress in the study, encourage members to participate in the closing prayer by praying out loud for each other and the requests given. Remind group members to pray for one another throughout the week.

Week 3
Isaac and Rebekah

Leader Prep

Bible Story Overview

We all want to leave a legacy, to be remembered for what we did and how we lived. Though Isaac is a supporting actor rather than a leading man in his family's story, his legacy is one of steady faith and trust in God. Once again, God is the main character in the story. God is always making Himself known, pursuing His people, and calling unlikely characters to lead and to bless others. This week, Isaac meets and marries Rebekah, a woman who demonstrates kindness and generosity. Like his parents, Isaac and Rebekah struggle to conceive. But Isaac is quick to pray, pleading with God for a child for his beloved Rebekah. And God provides. As Isaac and Rebekah search for their place in God's story, God is at work, always searching for and finding new ways to connect with His children.

Weekly Readings Recap

Review the key themes of the week:

Day 1: Although God does not ask Abraham to go through with the sacrifice of his son, Isaac's story establishes the type that will be realized in the fully completed sacrifice of a Son in Jesus. In an even broader context, the entire sacrificial system of the Old Testament serves as a type for the sacrifice of Jesus on the cross, told in the New Testament.

Day 2: Abraham sends his trusted servant, Eliezer, back to his homeland to search for a wife for Isaac from his own clan and tribe. Eliezer humbly gives praise to God for doing all the work, even though he could take credit for the long journey or boast in the wealth and power of the master who has sent him. This relationship between Abraham and his servant shows us a different kind of kinship, one formed through the journey they've been on together and the choice to be as close as family.

Day 3: We learn from Isaac and Rebekah's story that God is intimately interested in our desires, our needs, and our hopes. As we pray and seek His will, we must remember that it's not only about finding His path or plan for our lives but also about following His ways. He desires to bless us so that we may be a blessing to others.

Day 4: Like Abraham's family, we are formed by those who raise us and are deeply rooted in both their successes and mistakes. But God gives us a chance to start a new pattern in our generation.

Day 5: Having Isaac's name listed among the great stories of his people reminds us that we all have a place in history. Your name may not end up in history books, but you have a unique calling in your generation; and God is cheering you on as you fulfill it.

What You Will Need

- iPod or MP3 player with speakers or CD player and CD (see Preparing Your Hearts and Minds)
- *Broken and Blessed* DVD and DVD player
- Stick-on nametags and markers
- Each group member will need an item (or picture of an item) that she inherited from a previous generation in the family. (Send a reminder.)

Session Objective

Today you will help the women in your group discover their faith heritage and consider the legacy of faith they'll leave for future generations.

Session Outline

Preparing Your Hearts and Minds (2 minutes)

To help the women disconnect from the outside world and center their hearts on God, play a quiet, meaningful song as they are gathering. After the song has ended, pray the following opening prayer or a prayer of your own.

Loving God,
Thank You for Your awesome blessings in our lives. Thank You for
giving good gifts to Your children. Help us to trust in Your providence
and goodness. Illuminate the Scriptures and speak to our hearts in our
time together. In Jesus' name we pray. Amen.

Getting to Know Each Other (3-5 minutes)

Hand out nametags and markers and ask participants to write their names and wear the nametags for the session. Then have the women divide into pairs or small groups to discuss the following questions:

- Who would you say left a legacy of faith for you to carry on?
- What did you learn about God from him or her?
- What kind of faith legacy do you hope to leave for your family?

After a couple of minutes, come back together as a full group and have the pairs or groups share the highlights from their conversations.

Video (25-30 minutes)

Play the Week 3 video segment on the DVD. Invite participants to complete the Video Viewer Guide for Week 3 in the participant book as they watch.

Group Discussion (20-25 minutes)

Note that more discussion points and questions have been provided than you will have time to include. Before the session, select those you want to cover, and put a check mark beside them. Questions highlighted in bold are from the participant book. (In some instances, changes have been made, indicated with brackets, so that the questions make sense when read aloud to the group.) For these questions, you may want to invite participants to share the answers they wrote in their books.

1. When we read the story of Abraham walking with Isaac to Mount Moriah to lay him on an altar as a sacrifice, we imagine Abraham's anguish. But we need to remember that Isaac was a boy—old enough to know what was going on. (Day 1)
    - What do you think Isaac might have been thinking as this scene unfolded?
    - What did he learn about the faith of his father?
    - What did he learn about God?

- **In what ways do you think Abraham and Isaac's relationship might have changed after their mountaintop experience?**

2. Have participants review their notes from Day 1.
   - What did you discover about the way some Old Testament stories are connected to Christ's experiences?
   - How is Isaac's experience at Mount Moriah similar to the story of Jesus' baptism?

3. Our family of origin is the family we're born into; our family of destination is the family we marry into; and our family of choice is our most trusted and kindred friendships. (Day 2)
   - Who was Eliezer? Why was he so significant to Isaac's family?
   - How have persons in your family of choice influenced your future for good?
   - Have someone read Genesis 24:3-27. Describe what we learn of Eliezer's character in these verses.
   - **Is there someone you would trust to make a decision for you as significant as the one Abraham entrusts to this friend?**

4. Eliezer had a great responsibility. Abraham was trusting him to find a match for Isaac. Eliezer knew that he needed God's presence and wisdom for the search. (Day 3)
   - When have you been faced with a task too great for your own wisdom or strength?
   - **Is prayer your first stop or last resort [in your problem solving], or does it fall somewhere in between?**
   - When have you felt the power of God's presence as you made big decisions?

5. Read this passage aloud: "Rather than trying to get others to measure up to our expectations, berating them with our words, or trying to manipulate them with our disapproval, we should focus on our own behaviors. After all, there's only one person you can change, and that's yourself. All of our friendships and family relationships would probably improve if we followed Rebekah's example of showering others with kindness." (Day 3)
   - Have someone read Genesis 24:15-20. How did Rebekah display kindness and generosity?
   - How have you seen kindness improve relationships in your own life?
   - What are some things that keep us from showering others with kindness?

6. Although when we first meet Rebekah, she is willing to go above and beyond, showing unimaginable generosity for a stranger, later when it comes to her own family, she trades her generosity for stinginess. As her twin boys are growing up, she somehow gets the idea that she must love and favor one of them over the other. (Video)
   • What is scarcity? How does this mistaken notion lead to favoritism?
   • In the video, we heard about John Ortberg's concept of "sunset fatigue"— not having enough left at the end of the day for those we love. When have you experienced sunset fatigue? What is the answer or remedy?
   • Have you known those who play favorites—whether consciously or sub-consciously—according to how others satisfy their appetites or meet their needs? Have you ever been guilty of this yourself?
   • How is it possible to live out of God's abundance, loving others uncondi-tionally and generously?

7. God calls us to bless those within our family circle. (Day 3)
   • **Has there been a time when you felt that you received a blessing from your family?**
   • **Has there been a time when you gave a family member your blessing in some way?**

8. Similar to His promises to Abraham, God speaks to Isaac about the bless-ings he will see and the generations who will be blessed through him. (Day 4)
   • Review your notes from Day 4. What are the similarities of God's promise to Abraham and God's promise to Isaac?
   • **How have you experienced inherited blessings? What choices made by your family in previous generations have affected the richness of your life?**

9. Isaac was formed by the faith of his father, Abraham. He learned to build an altar to God regardless of the circumstances. We too are formed by both the mistakes and the faith of our families. The good news is that we get to build upon or start a new generation of faithfulness and worship regard-less of our circumstances. Our faith today can bless generations to come. (Day 4)
   • How have you been formed by the faith of others?
   • How are others formed by your faith?
   • What faith-based patterns can you begin today that will bring not only blessings to you today but also blessings to future generations in your family?

10. Isaac's story is sandwiched between the more prominent biblical stories of his father, Abraham, and his son Jacob. However, that doesn't make his story any less significant. He is a supporting character who serves a purpose in history—a purpose that is not diminished by the faith that comes before him or the drama that comes after him. (Day 5)
    • Who are the supporting characters in your family, the ones who may be more "behind the scenes" but who play an important role?
    • Isaac and Rebekah struggled to conceive as did Isaac's father, Abraham, and his mother, Sarah. Remember that Abraham and Sarah schemed to have a child through their servant Hagar. What does Isaac do when his wife cannot conceive? **According to Genesis 25:21, what is Isaac's response to the crisis?**

11. Review the teaching about Generation, Degeneration, and Regeneration in Day 5.
    • How can the big-picture view of Genesis be described by generation, degeneration, and regeneration?
    • How is this the cycle of our life with God through Jesus Christ?
    • **What have you learned from the seasons of generation, degeneration, and regeneration in your life?**
    • **Which season would you say you are in today?**

12. Wrap up Group Discussion with these questions:
    • What did you discover about brokenness and blessing this week?
    • What did you learn this week about God? About yourself?
    • How have you experienced God searching for you, never giving up in His pursuit of your heart?

*Act On It (10 minutes)

If you are meeting for 90 minutes, ask everyone to turn to a neighbor and talk about one or more of the following challenges from the Act On It section of the weekly readings:

Day 2: Share about some of the people in your family of choice who have been blessings in your life and how they have blessed you.

Day 3: Share about writing a letter to a young person. What kinds of things did you write or share with him or her? Were you surprised by any of your own thoughts or advice?

Day 5: Share about drawing your life map. Where did you see God's presence in all of those stages?

NOTES

*Group Activity (15 minutes)

If you are meeting for 90 minutes, have each woman show the group the item (or picture of an item) that she inherited from a previous generation. If group members couldn't bring an item or picture, they may simply describe something they've inherited. Invite them to talk about how it has been passed down through their family and why it is meaningful.

After everyone has shared, discuss the non-material things your families have passed down to you. Ask: *What have you inherited from your family? What do you hope those who come after will inherit from you?*

Closing Prayer (3 minutes)

As you end your session, make any announcements or review any details or dates regarding the group mission project. Close the session by taking personal prayer requests from group members and leading the group in prayer. Encourage members to participate in the closing prayer by praying out loud for each other and the requests given. Remind group members to pray for one another throughout the week.

Week 4
Jacob and Esau

Leader Prep

Bible Story Overview

This week we looked at the story of a family whose practices of favoritism poisoned the relationship between the two sons and led to full-blown sibling rivalry. The story of Jacob and Esau reads like a juicy soap opera of jealousy, deception, trickery, and hatred. Where it differs from most soaps, however, is in the reconciliation. Thankfully, this feud doesn't last forever. After Jacob steals everything Esau should rightfully inherit—his father's blessing and his birthright as the firstborn son—the brothers go their separate ways for many years only to later find a path to reconciliation. Through it all, God's patience, grace, and love overflow to all. This story of a family that withholds acceptance and treats love as though it is a scarce commodity makes it even clearer that our heavenly Father lavishes us with the tenderness and affection that we both need and crave.

Another thing we learn from this story is the power of a spoken blessing in our lives. Speaking blessings is one way for us to pass on our faith to future generations as well as be a blessing to those with whom we come in contact every day.

Weekly Readings Recap

Review the key themes of the week:

Day 1: From their earliest days (beginning in utero), Jacob and Esau's relationship is filled with conflict and strife. Because they are twins, we might expect them to be similar; but they are different in every way. Yet they are not solely to blame for the family fight that develops. Their parents set the stage for the ongoing competition and conflict that characterizes their sons' lives.

Day 2: Like Esau, we despise our birthright when we wish God had given us someone else's blessings. One of the best antidotes for comparison is thankfulness. If we are looking at our own gifts from God, it is difficult to have an eye on someone else's. Rather than focusing on what we don't have, God wants us to thank Him daily for the blessings He has placed in our lives.

Day 3: In Chapter 27 of Genesis, we find Jacob stooping to his lowest point. When he swiped Esau's birthright, he at least met his brother face-to-face and got his consent, no matter how underhanded his dealings were. Now Jacob deceives his own elderly and dying father. One of the greatest blessings we can give to those we love is the example of our own integrity.

Day 4: Jacob and Esau had a preoccupation with blessing based on their understanding of blessing as an incredibly powerful and meaningful act. They grasp what you and I should note: God wants us to give and receive meaningful blessings as part of our most significant relationships. And the good news is that blessings are not a limited resource.

Day 5: God reveals Himself in the faces of those who offer forgiveness. When we are called to forgive others, our actions can reflect God's face and God's love.

What You Will Need

- iPod or MP3 player with speakers or CD player and CD (see Preparing Your Hearts and Minds)
- *Broken and Blessed* DVD and DVD player
- Stick-on nametags and markers

Session Objective

Today you will help the women in your group explore favoritism in families and discover that our heavenly Father shows no favoritism; we are all afforded His tenderness and affection.

Session Outline

Preparing Your Hearts and Minds (2 minutes)

To help the women disconnect from the outside world and center their hearts on God, play a quiet, meaningful song as they are gathering. After the song has ended, pray the opening prayer below or a prayer of your own.

> *Heavenly Father,*
> *We confess that sometimes we look around and want what others have. We feel a lack of contentment for whatever reason and blame it on what we don't have when we have all we need in You. Help us to discover that You are impartial in Your love. Your tender mercies are available equally to all of us. Help us to claim Your promises and live into the story You are writing in us. In Jesus' name we pray. Amen.*

Getting to Know Each Other (3-5 minutes)

Hand out nametags and markers and ask participants to write their names and wear the nametags for the session. Then have the women divide into smaller groups to discuss the following questions:

- What kind of sibling rivalry occurs in your family?
- When do you feel most content? When do you feel discontent?

After a couple of minutes, come back together as a full group and have the groups share the highlights from their conversations.

Video (25-30 minutes)

Play the Week 4 video segment on the DVD. Invite participants to complete the Video Viewer Guide for Week 4 in the participant book as they watch.

Group Discussion (20-25 minutes)

Note that more discussion points and questions have been provided than you will have time to include. Before the session, select those you want to cover, and put a check mark beside them. Questions in bold are from the participant book. (In some instances, changes have been made, indicated with brackets, so that the questions make sense when read aloud to the group.) For these questions, you may want to invite participants to share answers they wrote in their books.

1. Jacob and Esau demonstrate for us one of the oldest and most colorful sibling rivalries in history. What began in utero carried on into adulthood, giving birth to jealousy, deception, bitterness, and separation. (Day 1 and Video)
   - What did you learn this week about Jacob and Esau's relationship?
   - How do their names describe their character and personalities?
   - Have you ever seen a family with siblings as different and antagonistic toward each other as Jacob and Esau? What was their dispute?

2. The story of Jacob and Esau demonstrates for us how two people who come from the same mix of DNA, share the same womb, and grow up in the same household can be so very different. From the beginning, parents have wondered how their children can be so different. But God makes each of us unique, and we can celebrate the fact that God knows and loves each of us as distinct individuals. (Day 1)
   - **How are you both like and different from other members of your family?**
   - **Read Matthew 10:28-31. How do these verses show you that God knows and values you personally?**
   - What would you say is required to bring family feuds to an end?

3. Siblings are masters of comparison. Early on, they learn about the mathematical concepts of "greater than" and "less than" by carefully watching out for who has more. His piece of brownie was *greater than* my piece. The time I got to spend in the bathroom was *less than* her time. He's taking up *greater than* his half of the back seat. Jacob and Esau demonstrate the urge between siblings to compete with each other. (Day 2 and Video)
   - When and how have you experienced or observed sibling rivalry in your family? What was the rivalry about?
   - What do you think was the root of the rivalry between Jacob and Esau?
   - **Have you ever compared your life to a friend's—either when you were growing up or in recent years? What was it about this person's life that seemed so appealing?**
   - Why do you think we are so prone to compete with others and to covet others' possessions, praise, acquisition, or reward?

4. Jacob is not completely to blame in this saga, because we see that Esau despises his birthright. Like Esau, we often are willing to trade our birthright—to give away our own gifts for the desire for what we see in someone else's hand. (Day 2 and Video)
   - In what ways have you traded in your birthright—overlooking your own gifts and abilities because of your desire to have those of someone else?
   - Why do you think we often find ourselves wishing we were like someone

else rather than appreciating the unique individuals that God has made us to be?

- How does comparing our blessings to others' keep us from seeing the blessings God is pouring into our own lives?
- How does the story of Fred Evans (video) inspire you to bless others in some way?

5. Both brothers eventually get what they want, but neither is ever truly satisfied. Esau's bowl of food will satisfy for only a time, and he will be hungry again, this time without an inheritance. Jacob's newly acquired birthright is the beginning of an underhanded series of events that will cause so much turmoil in the family that he will have to run away, making it impossible for him to enjoy the land, inheritance, and leadership he has seized. The competition between these two brothers winds up wounding their souls and damaging their relationship. (Day 2 and Video)
- Have someone read Genesis 25:29-34. Why do you think Esau was so nonchalant about his birthright?
- **Have you ever been tempted in the moment by something that you knew would jeopardize something more important in the long run? If so, what happened?**
- In our instant-gratification culture, how can we avoid trading significance for momentary wants?
- How has competition damaged relationships in your life?

6. One of the best antidotes for comparison is thankfulness. If we are looking at our own gifts from God, it is difficult to have an eye on someone else's. (Day 2)
- How does thankfulness keep us from comparison and discontent and greed?
- What has God done in your life that you wouldn't trade for anything?

7. The details of God's promises in Abraham, Isaac, and Jacob's story include land possession and offspring, but God's presence with them is the most important promise God made to them. Their legacy would include land and descendants; but even more important, their legacy is being tuned into God's presence all along the way. God makes that same promise of His presence to us as well. (Day 3)
- How have you known the very real and constant presence of God?
- When have you been distracted from God's presence by focusing on the details of a particular situation?
- What can you do to pass on a legacy of recognizing and experiencing God's faithful presence?

8. Jacob wanted to get ahead and would stop at nothing to get what he wanted. He was a bit of a mama's boy and even had his mom scheming to help him cheat, steal, and connive. Of course, she loved him dearly and wanted to see him achieve his dreams. (Day 3)
   - Do you have any sympathy for Rebekah's motives? Why or why not?
   - **When have you gone to great lengths to promote or defend a loved one? Did this experience cause you to compromise your integrity in any way, or was it an opportunity for you to demonstrate the love and character of Christ?**
   - How is living with integrity a blessing to others?

9. The concept of having only one blessing to pass on might seem foreign to us today. There are four timeless aspects or characteristics of blessing: *Blessing teaches us that the spoken word has power. Blessing starts with God. Blessing is intergenerational. Blessing is contagious.* (Day 4)
   - **What does Romans 8:28 say is God's goal for those who love Him?**
   - How have spoken blessings been powerful in your life?
   - How have you witnessed or been affected by contagious blessings?
   - **How can you be contagious with your blessings, sharing them with others?**

10. Years later, Jacob rightly has lost hope that he would ever reconcile with his brother. But God moves in the hearts of these brothers. Esau surprises Jacob with forgiveness and generosity. Though Jacob stole everything Esau would inherit, the years between the betrayal and the reconciliation have softened both of them. Their reunion is tender and full of grace and mercy. (Day 5)
    - When have you deserved anger but received grace?
    - Have someone read Genesis 33:10. **When Esau forgives Jacob, to what does Jacob compare seeing his brother's face?**
    - How does this moment of healing between the brothers demonstrate for us the heart of God?
    - How is Jacob and Esau's story similar to the parable of the prodigal son?
    - **In the prodigal story, do you identify more with the son who has run away and returned home or with the son who has faithfully served?**

11. Wrap up Group Discussion with these questions:
    - What did you discover about brokenness and blessing this week from Jacob and Esau's story?
    - What did you learn this week about God? About yourself?
    - How have you recognized blessing in your own life this week?

*Act On It (10 minutes)

If you are meeting for 90 minutes, ask everyone to turn to a neighbor and talk about one or more of the following challenges from the Act On It section of the weekly readings:

Day 2: Share your experience of keeping a gratitude list. Did this practice help you to appreciate the special blessings of each day?

Day 3: Share your experience of giving the blessing of good character this week. In what ways were you able to be a blessing of good character to others?

Day 4: Share about writing a letter of blessing to a loved one. Whom did you choose? What surprised you as you wrote the letter? Were there any recurring themes?

*Group Activity (15 minutes)

If you are meeting for 90 minutes, have the women divide into pairs. Remind the group of the power of a spoken blessing and invite the pairs to speak a word of blessing into each other's lives. Invite each woman to share with her partner an area in which she needs a blessing—it may be finances, a relationship, a situation in her life needing hope, and so on. For example, someone might share that she needs a blessing of hope because her mother is fighting cancer. Her partner might say a blessing such as, "May God bless you with great hope and comfort as you fight alongside your mother in her battle with cancer."

After the women are finished, come back together for a time of prayer.

Closing Prayer (3 minutes)

As you end your session, make any announcements or review any details or dates regarding the group mission project. Close the session by taking personal prayer requests from group members and leading the group in prayer. Encourage members to participate in the closing prayer by praying out loud for each other and the requests given. Remind group members to pray for one another throughout the week.

Week 5
Rachel and Leah

Leader Prep

Bible Story Overview

This week we looked at another classic example of sibling rivalry, this time a tale of two sisters. Rachel and Leah not only grew up in the same flawed family but even married the same man, creating a large dysfunctional brood of their own! The insights we catch from the story of these sisters and their struggle for love should propel us in a direction opposite from theirs, encouraging us to give rather than take, to love rather than despise, and to see family members as close allies and team members rather than competitors.

Weekly Readings Recap

Review the key themes of the week:

Day 1: Jacob encounters Rachel, who would become the love of his life, at a well. Another woman in the New Testament encounters the true source of love and life, Jesus, at a well. Like these two women, we all have the desire to find the satisfaction of true love. If we look to Jesus for love, we will find His love becomes a spring of life within us, welling up and spilling out onto others.

Day 2: The morning after his wedding night, Jacob realizes he has been given the wrong sister. When Jacob approaches Laban in his anger, Jacob sees his own flaws reflected in his Uncle Laban. He experiences firsthand the kind of pain and disappointment that he caused to his own brother. And Rachel and Leah are set up for a future life together under the same roof married to the same man—a life in which they will continue to compete for attention, affection, and love. Yet God continues to walk beside them.

Day 3: In yet another scenario of infertility, Rachel struggles to become pregnant while her sister Leah gives Jacob several children. She is one of several women in this family who would share the struggle. While we don't know why the women struggled with infertility, we can know for sure that God's faithfulness is bigger than our afflictions and that God uses our barrenness and times of waiting to prepare us for the blessings to come.

Day 4: From the beginning of their story, it is very clear that Jacob is in love with Rachel but has to take Leah as part of the package. Rachel may be the one loved best by Jacob, but she is unable to have children, a fact that causes her great pain and distress. Rachel and Leah remind us that God created families to operate as teams, not as competitors.

Day 5: Jacob finally gets what he wants, his family heading back to his home. Although Jacob and Laban have had their differences and, in many ways, have met their conniving match in each other, they reconcile and make a covenant together. The ability to move past the hurts that other family members have caused us is something that many of us struggle to attain. But God wants us to lift up our hurts and concerns to Him so that He can heal and renew us as we move forward.

What You Will Need

- iPod or MP3 player with speakers or CD player and CD (see Preparing Your Hearts and Minds)
- *Broken and Blessed* DVD and DVD player
- Stick-on nametags and markers

Session Objective

Today you will help the women in your group discover that jealousy and competition only complicate matters. God has blessed each of us immensely, and we have an opportunity to be a blessing to others.

Session Outline

Preparing Your Hearts and Minds (2 minutes)

To help the women disconnect from the outside world and center their hearts on God, play a quiet, meaningful song as they are gathering. After the song has ended, pray the opening prayer below or a prayer of your own.

> *Heavenly Father,*
> *We confess that we are often jealous of others. We are not unlike Jacob and Laban, scheming to get what we want. And often we are like Rachel, growing impatient for Your promises to become reality and trying to make things happen on our own. Other times we are like Leah, flaunting what we have in the face of those who have not, because of our insecurity. Forgive us, God. Illuminate Your Word to us now and show us Your path. In Jesus' name we pray. Amen.*

Getting to Know Each Other (3-5 minutes)

Hand out nametags and markers and ask participants to write their names and wear the nametags for the session. Then have the women divide into smaller groups to discuss the following questions:

- What was the most deceitful thing you ever pulled off as a young person?
- On a scale of 1-7, how competitive would you say you generally are?

After a couple of minutes, come back together as a full group and have the groups share the highlights from their conversations.

Video (25-30 minutes)

Play the Week 5 video segment on the DVD. Invite participants to complete the Video Viewer Guide for Week 5 in the participant book as they watch.

Group Discussion (20-25 minutes)

Note that more discussion points and questions have been provided than you will have time to include. Before the session, select those you want to cover, and put a check mark beside them. Questions in bold are from the participant book. (In some instances, changes have been made, indicated with brackets, so that the questions make sense when read aloud to the group.) For these questions, you may want to invite participants to share the answers they wrote in their books.

1. Jacob and Rachel's love story begins at a well, similar to the story of Abraham's assistant finding a wife for his son, Isaac, at a well. Remember that Rebekah was chosen because she offered to water all of Eliezer's camels. Now, at this well, it's Jacob who offers to help water Rachel's sheep. He is clearly smitten with her from the minute he sees her. (Day 1)
   • **Though it may seem strange to us that many of the Bible's love stories began through arranged marriage and even encounters at a well, do you think any of our culture's courting habits might have seemed alien to Jacob and his contemporaries? If so, which ones?**
   • Review your notes from Day 1. How does this meeting at a well compare to Jesus' encounter many years later with a woman at Jacob's Well?

2. The woman at the well in John 4 looked in all the wrong places to find real love. Only when she met Jesus at a well did she understand that nothing would satisfy her need for love except His perfect love. (Day 1)
   • **When have you searched for happiness in something that did not satisfy?**
   • Read aloud John 4:13-14. **How have you found satisfaction in Christ?**
   • What does it mean that Christ's love spills out of our hearts onto others?

3. Rachel and Leah give us another episode of sibling rivalry. Rachel was the pretty one, and Leah was the one we might describe today as having a "nice personality." Laban tricks Jacob into marrying Leah first and then makes a deal for him to finally get Rachel as his bride. Uncle Laban uses "the old switcheroo" that Jacob practiced on his brother, and now the older to younger thievery has been reversed. (Day 2 and Video)
   • How do you think Rachel felt knowing she was the one Jacob wanted?
   • How do you think Leah must have felt knowing she was second best compared to Rachel?
   • When have you felt favored?
   • When have you felt second best?
   • Jacob is confronted with his own flaw when his uncle deceives him. **Can you think of something that irritates you in other people that is actually a flaw of your own? Read Luke 6:42. What was Jesus' advice to us when we notice flaws in others?**
   • Why is it so much easier to point out other people's flaws than to work on our own?

4. One of the most difficult topics to discuss, especially among women, is infertility. Often women struggle in private, ashamed or despairing that their bodies are not cooperating with their dreams. It seems ironic that God would promise innumerable offspring to Abraham's descendants

when the first three matriarchs of the Old Testament struggle to conceive. God's great promise of abundance to this family is instantly followed by three generations of great barriers to that promise. (Day 3)

- Why do you think barrenness followed a promise of abundance?
- What do you think Sarah, Rebekah, and Rachel learned about God when they saw their promise fulfilled?

5. We've all experienced times of waiting. At one time or another and in one way or another, we've all felt "barren," waiting on God's timing or plan to be revealed in our lives. The good news is that God uses our barrenness and times of waiting to prepare us for the blessings to come. Even now God is working and molding us into the image of His Son as we wait on His return and the restoration of all things. (Day 3)

- **When have you prayed for something that was a deep desire of your heart, and what was the outcome?**
- How have you learned about God and God's faithfulness in barren times?
- How does God use our times of waiting to prepare us for blessings?

6. Rachel and Leah begin a competition to see who can give Jacob the most sons. Of course, Rachel thinks she will never win this game because she has yet to have a child of her own. So she uses Jacob's grandmother's tactic of sending in a maidservant to bear a child for her. Soon Leah follows suit. The two sisters use their children to keep score in their rivalry. This kind of ranking-by-children still goes on today. (Day 4 and Video)

- Review your notes from Day 4. What did you learn about the names that Leah and Rachel chose for their children? How did even their names speak to the competitive nature of their relationship?
- **What are some ways you have seen parents comparing their children? How do you think this affects children and families?**

7. When family members compete and act as rivals, they decline the joy of winning together, losing together, hurting together, and celebrating together. This was true for Jacob and Esau as well as for Rachel and Leah, and it would be true for all twelve of Jacob's children, who would turn on their brother Joseph. What was true then is still true today: competition and comparison are toxic elements in our lives and families. (Day 4 and Video)

- How do family feuds steal the joy from a family?
- **How have you experienced or witnessed competition in your own family?** What have been some of the toxic effects of competition and comparison in your family?
- How have you experienced or witnessed unity in your family? What blessings have you observed as a result of this unity?

• Have someone read 1 Corinthians 6:19-20. How can these verses encourage us to stop comparing ourselves to others?

8. You may be privileged to have one or two sisters related by blood, but you are surrounded by sisters who are related by the blood of Christ. Rather than treat our sisters as our rivals we should appreciate them as gifts intended to enrich and bless our lives. We all need warmth and love and support from the women around us. (Video)
   • Why do you think we women tend to treat other women as measuring sticks, comparing ourselves and determining how we measure up? What happens when we do this?
   • In what ways is sisterhood an asset that can't be counted, compared, or competed for? How has sisterhood been a blessing in your own life?

9. When the time came for Jacob to take his family and return to his homeland, there was one piece of baggage in the caravan that Jacob hadn't counted on. Before they left, Rachel had stolen her father's idols. Of all the things Laban could have missed when Jacob snuck away with his daughters, grandchildren, and much of his flock, he missed his idols the most. Laban shows us a clear picture of how we are prone to put idols in our lives, giving them a place of value over our family and over God himself. (Day 5)
   • **What are some of the things we tend to put above God as priorities or idols in our lives?**

10. Laban seemed to calm down after his strong reaction to Jacob sneaking away with his family and flock, and he and Jacob reconciled and made a covenant together. The ceremony of reconciliation included a promise not to harm each other further. We can't always count on others to make or fulfill such a promise, and God does not call us to put ourselves in harm's way by placing trust where none is deserved. But God does want us to lift up our hurts and concerns to Him so that He can heal and renew us as we move forward. (Day 5)
    • **Is there a family member or friend who is estranged from you or others because of a wrong committed in the past? How does that affect your relationship?**
    • **What would help you (and/or others) to be able to move past the hurt?**
    • When have you or others in your family experienced reconciliation after a long period of discord?
    • **What does Laban do in Genesis 31:55?**
    • How can you bless your family so that they know their worth to you?

11. Wrap up Group Discussion with these questions:
- What did you discover about brokenness and blessing this week?
- What did you learn this week about God? About yourself?
- How have you felt God working in you through the story of Rachel and Leah?

*Act On It (10 minutes)

If you are meeting for 90 minutes, ask everyone to turn to a neighbor and talk about one or more of the following challenges from the Act On It section of the weekly readings:

Day 2: Share about your experience of releasing your resentment toward someone. How does it feel to replace resentment with thanksgiving for God's goodness in both of your lives?

Day 3: Share an area of "barrenness" in your life right now. How are you waiting on God, and how do you think God is preparing you for what is to come?

Day 4: Share some of the ways that you can intentionally support and encourage your family of choice.

*Group Activity (15 minutes)

If you are meeting for 90 minutes, have the women divide into small groups. In light of the discussion about women who struggle with infertility, invite the groups to pray specifically for women—in your own Bible study group and/or in the circles of women you know—who are struggling with infertility (silently or publically) or who are somewhere in the adoption process. Or you might choose to pray for women—in your group or in your circles—who are struggling with other difficult family issues. Explain that this prayer time is not for gossip but for pleading with God on behalf of women who are struggling and waiting on God. Ask the women to pray boldly that these women may have their prayers answered.

After the women are finished, come back together for a time of closing prayer.

Closing Prayer (3 minutes)

As you end your session, make any announcements or review any details or dates regarding the group mission project. Close the session by taking personal prayer requests from group members and leading the group in prayer. Encourage members to participate in the closing prayer by praying out loud for each other and the requests given. Remind group members to pray for one another throughout the week.

Week 6
Joseph and His Brothers

Leader Prep

Bible Story Overview

Here we are at the last major Genesis family. Generation after generation, they have displayed more brokenness than overflowing blessings to those around them. Adam and Eve introduced brokenness into a perfect world; Abraham and Sarah struggled to trust God's promise; Isaac and Rebekah poisoned their family with favoritism; and the two sets of siblings—Jacob and Esau and Rachel and Leah—were dominated by competition and comparison. How will this family change the world when they need so much change? This pivotal generation of Jacob's sons faces the pressure to resolve some of the patterns that have trickled down through the family so that they can become an effective conduit for God's blessings. Yet they become so enraged with their brother Joseph that they scheme a fake murder, sell him into slavery, and lie to their father. Even so, blessing finds its way into the story. Joseph ultimately forgives his brothers, turning things around for their family and the future generations to come. In the final scene, Jacob speaks a blessing over his family, pointing to God's abundance in their lives.

Weekly Readings Recap

Review the key themes of the week:

Day 1: Between their father's preferential treatment and Joseph's dreaming and bragging, the brothers have plenty of reasons to develop a deep hatred for Joseph. Joseph's dreams of his family bowing and scraping have deeper meaning than anyone may have guessed. He will one day rule over a great number of people and save the lives of many; but he will have to wait until he is ready, allowing his character and trust in God to develop. When God wants us to accomplish big things for His kingdom, He must prepare in us big character to match big vision.

Day 2: Joseph goes from his comfortable family home to slave quarters and from the pit of a dungeon to second in command of a kingdom. But he doesn't let negative circumstances drive him to despair or success drive him to pride. His resilience makes him levelheaded in the midst of the changes, and his humility drives him to seek God at all times.

Day 3: When his brothers unknowingly stand in front of him, Joseph wrestles with the question of how to handle this reunion, since the decision between revenge and reconciliation lies completely in his hands. When we wrestle, as Joseph did, with how to react to those who've hurt us, God will give us the grace to respond not with our strength but with His.

Day 4: Joseph is the family member who breaks the family cycle and begins a new way of relating within the family. Whatever cycles have played out in your family in the past, you were not meant to stay in an ongoing cycle of defeat. God calls us to be new creations, to chart a new course as the first generation that chooses a new path.

Day 5: God transforms this family through Joseph. No longer will they be deceivers. No longer will they remain broken. Joseph has the power to change the script, and he does. He changes his family so that his family will change the world. We have our moments of brokenness, of course, but they are far overshadowed by God's continual blessings.

What You Will Need

- iPod or MP3 player with speakers or CD player and CD (see Preparing Your Hearts and Minds)
- *Broken and Blessed* DVD and DVD player
- Stick-on nametags and markers
- Small, square mirror for each participant (from a craft store)
- Bags of colored glass pieces (from a craft store)
- Craft glue

Session Objective

Today you will help the women in your group discover that nothing in this world can separate us from God and that He is calling us, His children, to be a blessing to the world.

Session Outline

Preparing Your Hearts and Minds (2 minutes)

To help the women disconnect from the outside world and center their hearts on God, play a quiet, meaningful song as they are gathering. After the song has ended, pray the opening prayer below or a prayer of your own.

> *Loving God,*
> *Help us to trust that there is nothing that can separate us from You. Help us to say yes when You call us to be a blessing. Pour out Your blessings on us and write the truth upon our hearts that we are blessed to be a blessing. We ask this in Jesus' name. Amen.*

Getting to Know Each Other (3-5 minutes)

Hand out nametags and markers and ask participants to write their names and wear the nametags for the session. Then have each woman turn to a neighbor to discuss the following questions:

- When have you had the perfect chance to give someone what she or he deserved but you chose grace instead? How difficult was that for you?
- When you think about being a blessing to the world, how do you imagine God might use you?

After a couple of minutes, come back together as a full group and have the women share highlights from their conversations.

Video (25-30 minutes)

Play the Week 6 video segment on the DVD. Invite participants to complete the Video Viewer Guide for Week 6 in the participant book as they watch.

Group Discussion (20-25 minutes)

Note that more discussion points and questions have been provided than you will have time to include. Before the session, select those you want to cover, and put a check mark beside them. Questions in bold are from the participant book. (In some instances, changes have been made, indicated with brackets, so that the questions make sense when read aloud to the group.) For these questions, you may want to invite participants to share the answers they wrote in their books.

1. To his brothers, Joseph is a mouthy teenager who is full of himself and receives too much attention from their father. Though Joseph's dreams of ruling over his family do have meaning, he is either naïve or intentionally confrontational in sharing them with his brothers. (Day 1 and Video)
   - Have someone read aloud Genesis 37:5-9. **If you were Joseph's brothers, how would you interpret the symbols in his dreams?**
   - Do you think Joseph was naïve or intentionally confrontational in sharing his dreams? Why?
   - What do you think you would have said to Joseph if you were a sibling listening to him go on about his "visions"?

2. While it is true that Joseph's dreams one day will become realities, Joseph isn't quite ready for the big show. God has some work to do in him to prepare him for the blessing he will become. (Day 1)
   - **Can you think of any dreams that God had to prepare you for before entrusting them to you?**
   - **What has happened in your life that you wouldn't have been prepared to handle if it had taken place earlier?**

3. Because of their hatred for Joseph, the brothers sell him to a band of slave traders, and he finds himself a slave in Egypt. Once again he finds himself victimized when he is falsely accused of sexual harassment. Yet he continually shows character and perseverance. Unlike his father, Joseph does not deceive others or manipulate situations for his own gain. (Day 2)
   - Joseph's father, Jacob, was a schemer and a manipulator. How do you think he might have reacted if he were in Joseph's situation?
   - How did Joseph respond to the terrible acts committed against him?
   - **How do the words of Colossians 3:22-25 describe Joseph's attitude?**
   - **What can help you to demonstrate character and perseverance despite difficult circumstances?**
   - When has suffering produced character in you?

4. Joseph rises to power because of his ability to interpret the Pharaoh's dreams. He displays integrity and good will all the way from his slave's quarters to the Pharaoh's side. Wherever Joseph goes, God blesses him; and Joseph doesn't hesitate to give credit to God. Sometimes, like Joseph, we must wait on our dreams; and as we wait, we can always give thanks to God for His faithfulness. God is not only with us at all times; He blesses us at all times. Nothing ever separates us from his love. (Day 2 and Video)
   - Have some volunteers read Genesis 39:7-9, 40:8, and 41:16. **How does Joseph give glory to God in each of these situations?**

- How easy or difficult is it for you to give God the glory when good things happen? What about when not-so-good things happen?
- **Have you ever witnessed the death of one of your dreams? Have you ever seen a new dream emerge that is better than what you had hoped in the beginning?**
- **How is God currently working to bring His dreams into reality in your life?**
- What did you write in the blank on your Video Viewer Guide? "For I am convinced that _____ cannot separate me from the love of God that is in Christ Jesus."

5. Joseph has great professional success and prepares Egypt for a famine that only he has the foresight to plan for. Because of this, he finds himself in the position of ordering food rations for refugees to Egypt—among them his brothers. (Day 3 and Video)
   - Have someone read Genesis 42:8-9, 24. **What is Joseph's outward reaction?** What is the reaction his brothers cannot see?
   - When have you had to temper your emotions in a moment and then escape to privacy to let out your true feelings?
   - Why do you think the brothers didn't recognize Joseph?

6. God's children sometimes do terrible things to one another. Like Joseph, all of us have probably been wounded either by the carelessness of people we love or even by their outright cruelty. And like him, we've likely been tempted to take revenge. God is gentle with our wounds but also gives us guidance on how to handle the wounds inflicted by others. (Day 3 and Video)
   - Have four volunteers read Matthew 5:43-45, Proverbs 29:21-23, and Matthew 18:21-22. **How does God call us to respond when we are hurt?**
   - Why do you think some wounds continue to sting even years later?
   - How do we know that Joseph struggled with the desire to take revenge—to treat his brothers as he had been treated?
   - When did the turning point come for Joseph? What brought it about?
   - Do you think Joseph was able to truly forgive and forget? Why or why not?

7. Joseph pursues a path of peace for the future of this family. For generations this family has lived with a script of competition and revenge. Their father, Jacob, and his brother, Esau, had an encounter of forgiveness, but we have no record of their relationship after that moment to know if the relationship was restored. Unlike his ancestors, Joseph chooses to forgive his brothers and live in peace with them. (Day 4 and Video)
   - How was Joseph positioned to change the future of his family story? What did he do to bring about this new direction? How difficult do you think this was for him and why?

- Have you experienced or witnessed a reconciliation and restoration of a relationship in your family? What were some characteristics of that healing?
- Have someone read 2 Corinthians 5:16-20. **As a new creation in Christ, how can you offer the message of reconciliation—for others to be reconciled to God and to one another?**
- Have someone read Genesis 49:1. **Whom does Jacob call to his bedside?** What is the significance of this? What does this mean about the depth of transformation in this family?

8. Jacob is blessing Joseph by blessing his sons. Loving parents understand what a joy and blessing it is when their children are happy and at peace. For Jacob to pass on a blessing to Joseph's sons is the best gift Joseph could receive. (Day 5)
   - **What are some of the blessings you wish for your children or for the young people in your family or community of faith?**
   - Review your notes from Day 5. What is significant about Jacob's adoption of Ephraim and Manasseh?

9. When we read the story of Jacob adopting Ephraim and Manasseh as his own sons, it teaches us something about another adoption that the Bible will introduce years later. The adoption is our own. Because of what God has done through His Son, Jesus, you and I have been welcomed into this amazing family. (Day 5)
   - Review your notes from Day 5. How are we adopted into the family of God?
   - What does it mean to you to know that you are part of God's family?

10. God loves to start with one family to spread His blessings out to others, to make them blessed to be a blessing. But He also loves to start with one person in that family to bring about change for many generations through the transformation of just one person. (Video)
    - Who is the "Joseph" in your family?
    - How might God be calling you to be the "Joseph" in your family?

11. Wrap up Group Discussion with these questions:
    - How would you summarize what you have learned through this study about God? About yourself?
    - How is God calling you be a blessing to your family? To the world?
    - How might God want to use the brokenness in your life or your family to bless others?
    - How have you been blessed to be a blessing?

*Act On It (10 minutes)

If you are meeting for 90 minutes, ask everyone to turn to a neighbor and talk about one or more of the following challenges from the Act On It section of the weekly readings:

Day 1: Share any unfulfilled dreams in your life and how God may be preparing you for a future yet to come.

Day 4: What are some of the blessings that individual family members have brought to your family? What blessings from previous generations have trickled down to you?

Day 5: Talk about the ways churches care for one another. How might you participate in the care of your community? What can you do to support your family of faith locally and globally?

*Group Activity (15 minutes)

If you are meeting for 90 minutes, have the women sit at a table. Explain that they are going to make a small mosaic mirror to remember that God takes brokenness and turns it into blessing. Hand out the small, square mirrors, bags of colored glass pieces, and glue. Invite each woman to make a mosaic frame around the edge of the mirror by gluing glass pieces onto the mirror. Encourage them to remember that even when there is brokenness in our lives, God pours out His blessings on us, His children. Encourage them to remember when they look into their mirrors that the one they see is blessed beyond measure—blessed to be a blessing.

Closing Prayer (3 minutes)

As you end your session, make any final announcements or review final details regarding the group mission project. If you have been collecting items, remember to pray a blessing over them before sending them on.

Close the session by taking personal prayer requests from group members and leading the group in prayer. Thank the participants for making this journey together and challenge them to keep their eyes open for God's blessings in their lives as well as the ways that He can use them to be a blessing in their families and the world. End with this final blessing: *You are His. You are loved. You are blessed.*

Leaf
Pattern
(light green)

Tree Trunk
Pattern
(brown)

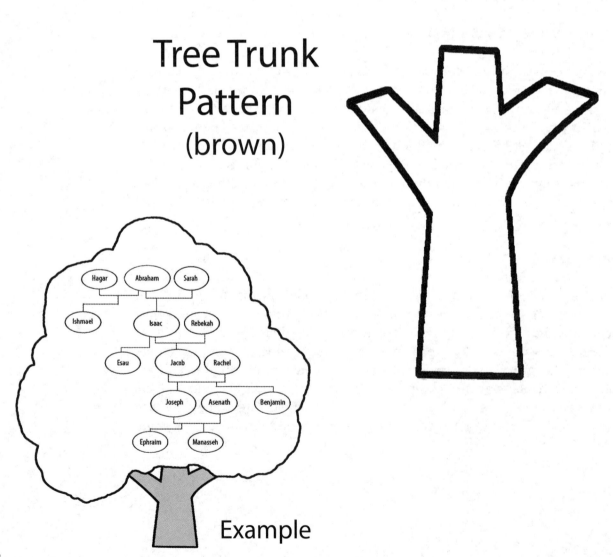

Example

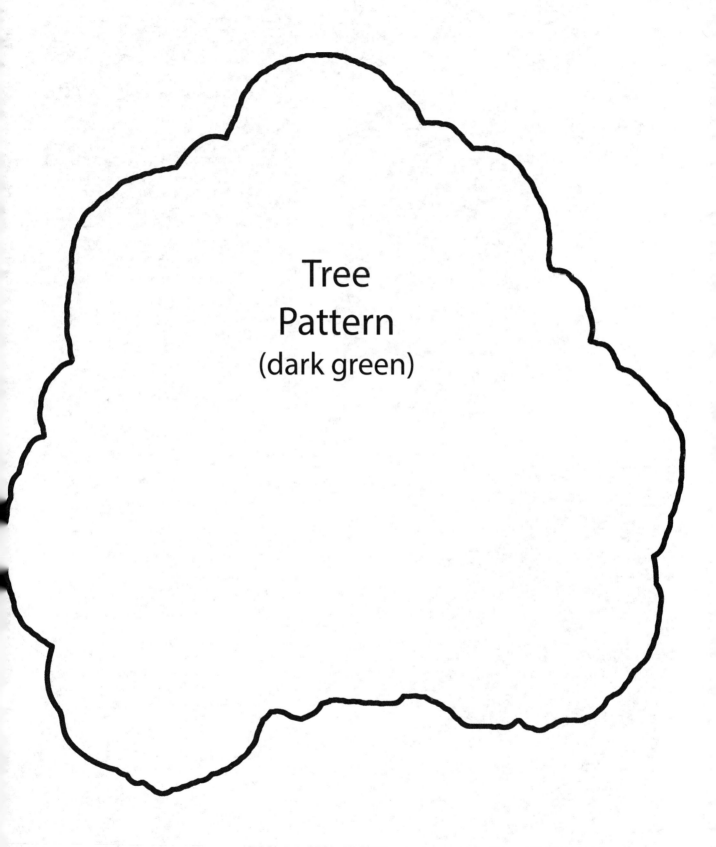

Tree
Pattern
(dark green)